ANIMAL LIFESTYLES

Divers

By Alison Ballance

Table of Contents

Dominie Press, Inc.

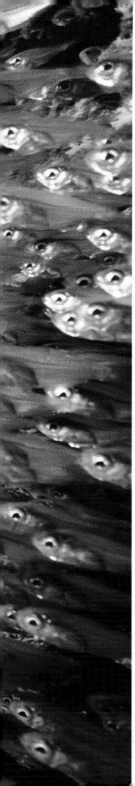

Introduction

When people go under water, they have to hold their breath. They also can use special **SCUBA** diving **equipment** to breathe for a few hours. People do not usually spend a lot of time in the water. When we do, we need special equipment to help us breathe and move around.

Many animals are much better at diving than we are. They spend most or all of their time in the water. Some animals can dive into the water and swim fast, but they are slow and **clumsy** when they are on land. In this book, we will look at some animals who dive.

Sperm Whales

Sperm whales dive very deep to hunt for food. Their powerful tails help **propel** them deep into the ocean. It is so dark at the bottom of the ocean that the whales use sound to find their way around, like a bat flying at night. A sperm whale can hold its breath for up to an hour.

The sperm whale has the largest brain of all animals. It can weigh 20 pounds. A human's brain weighs about three pounds.

Weddell Seals

Weddell seals live in Antarctica. **Scientists** have been studying the seals as they dive under the ice. They put tiny cameras on a seal's head so they can see how it hunts for fish. This does not hurt the seal, and it gives the scientists a lot of information.

Weddell seals come up for air through holes in the ice. They have strong front teeth so they can chew ice and stop the holes from icing over.

Elephant Seals

Elephant seals are world-record divers. They can dive deeper than a mile and hold their breath for up to two hours. It is very cold at the bottom of the ocean, so an elephant seal has a lot of **blubber** to keep it warm.

Elephant seals spend almost all their lives in the ocean. They are excellent swimmers, but on land they do not move very fast.

Diving Beetles

A diving beetle uses a tiny version of a SCUBA tank. When it is under water, it breathes from a bubble of air **trapped** under its wings. When the air runs out, the diving beetle floats to the surface and gets a new bubble.

Diving beetles use their strong, sharp jaws to catch prey. Their bite is very painful, even to people.

Marine Iguanas

Marine iguanas are the only lizards in the world that go into the ocean for food. They can dive for up to an hour. While they are under water, they scrape seaweed off the rocks with their teeth. They get very cold in the water, so they have to lie in the sun to warm up.

Marine iguanas have flat tails to help them swim, and long claws so they can hold on to rocks.

13

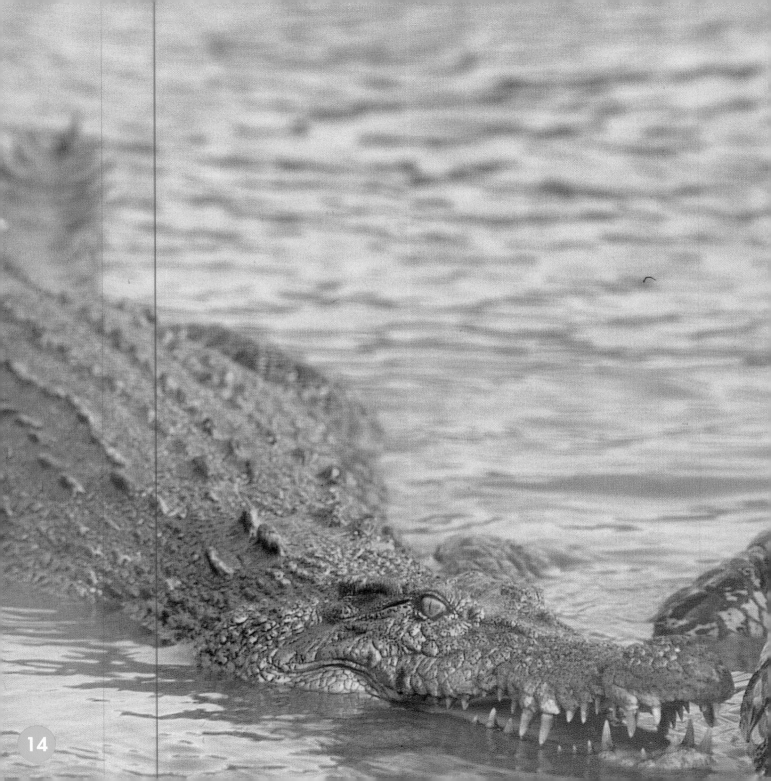

Crocodiles

Crocodiles have a special **heart** that helps them stay under water for a long time. While they are diving, their heart beats very slowly and only sends blood to important parts of the body, such as the brain. This means the crocodile uses much less **oxygen**.

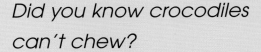

Did you know crocodiles can't chew?

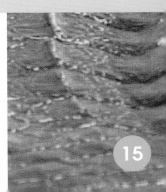

Gannets

Some seabirds are good high divers. Gannets **hover** over the ocean until they see a fish. Then they point their head down, tuck their wings in, and dive into the water. They can dive from 100 feet in the air. They hit the water so fast, they send up a big shower of spray.

Gannets have large webbed feet, which make them fast swimmers. But webbed feet are not good for walking on land. Gannets look clumsy when they walk.

Cormorants

Cormorants float on top of the water and look for fish. When they see a fish, they put their head under the water and give a strong kick with their legs to dive. They hold their breath and swim under water as they chase fish.

*Most birds have **hollow** bones to make them light, but a cormorant does not. Because they are heavier, it is harder for cormorants to fly, but it is easier for them to dive for food.*

Penguins

Penguins "fly" under water using their wings. They can dive hundreds of times in a day. They stay down until they run out of breath and then swim back to the surface to breathe.

*Every year, penguins lose all of their **insulating** feathers and then grow new ones. Penguins can't dive for three weeks during this time.*

Summary

Different animals dive in different ways. Seals use their powerful flippers to push them down into the ocean. Gannets dive from high in the air and fall into the ocean. Both of them dive for the same reason: to look for food.

Some animals that dive and swim, like whales, spend all of their lives in water. Others, like marine iguanas, go into the water only for food. Compared to animals who dive, people are not very good at staying in the water for very long, even with SCUBA tanks.

23

Glossary

blubber   a layer of thick fat in some animals

clumsy   awkward

equipment   special tools needed to do something

heart   the part of a body that pumps blood

hollow   empty inside

hover   to hold a position in the air

insulating   holding in heat

marine   coming from, or living in, the ocean

oxygen   an element of air that we breathe and need to live

propel   to push something forward

scientists   people who study science

SCUBA   a device that lets humans breathe under water

trapped   when something is held so it can't get away

Index